Dear Parents and Educators,

Welcome to Penguin Young Readers! A
know that each child develops at his or her
speech, critical thinking, and, of course, reading. Penguin Young
Readers recognizes this fact. As a result, each Penguin Young Readers
book is assigned a traditional easy-to-read level (1–4) as well as a
Guided Reading Level (A–P). Both of these systems will help you choose
the right book for your child. Please refer to the back of each book
for specific leveling information. Penguin Young Readers features
esteemed authors and illustrators, stories about favorite characters,
fascinating nonfiction, and more!

Hedge-Hedgey-Hedgehogs

LEVEL **2**

GUIDED
READING
LEVEL **H**

This book is perfect for a **Progressing Reader** who:
• can figure out unknown words by using picture and context clues;
• can recognize beginning, middle, and ending sounds;
• can make and confirm predictions about what will happen in the text; and
• can distinguish between fiction and nonfiction.

Here are some **activities** you can do during and after reading this book:
• Nonfiction: Nonfiction books deal with facts and events that are real.
  Talk about the elements of nonfiction. On a separate sheet of paper, write
  down what you learned about hedgehogs.
• Sight Words: Sight words are frequently used words that readers must
  know just by looking at them. They are known instantly, on sight. Knowing
  these words helps children develop into efficient readers. As you read the
  story, have the child point out the sight words below.

give	live	of	put	take
just	may	once	some	think

Remember, sharing the love of reading with a child is the best gift
you can give!

—Bonnie Bader, EdM
  Penguin Young Readers program

*Penguin Young Readers are leveled by independent reviewers applying the standards developed by Irene Fountas
and Gay Su Pinnell in *Matching Books to Readers: Using Leveled Books in Guided Reading*, Heinemann, 1999.

To Bailey, the best pet ever!—BB

PENGUIN YOUNG READERS
An Imprint of Penguin Random House LLC

Penguin supports copyright. Copyright fuels creativity, encourages diverse voices, promotes free speech, and creates a vibrant culture. Thank you for buying an authorized edition of this book and for complying with copyright laws by not reproducing, scanning, or distributing any part of it in any form without permission. You are supporting writers and allowing Penguin to continue to publish books for every reader.

Photo credits: cover: © Thinkstock/Carmelka; page 3: © Thinkstock/Carmelka; page 4: © Thinkstock/Eric Isselée; page 5: © Thinkstock/imegastocker; pages 6–7: © Thinkstock/Carmelka; page 8: (hedgehog and hand) © Thinkstock/praisaeng, (hedgehog in jar) © Thinkstock/ChrisPethick, (lying hedgehog) © Thinkstock/Azaliya; page 9: © Thinkstock/MikeLane45; pages 10–11: (hedgehog) © Thinkstock/Eric Isselée, (snail) © Thinkstock/Vladifot; page 12: (hedgehog) © Thinkstock/bazilfoto, (bug) © Thinkstock/DenBoma; page 13: © Thinkstock/Carmelka; page 14: © Thinkstock/Carmelka; page 15: © Thinkstock/borzywoj; pages 16–17: © Thinkstock/Ornitolog82; page 18: (hedgehog) © Thinkstock/zorandimzr, (cage) © Thinkstock/Beth Van trees; page 19: © Thinkstock/Valengilda; page 20: © Thinkstock/mbolina; page 21: © Thinkstock/Carmelka; page 22: © Thinkstock/MikeLane45; page 23: © Thinkstock/Carmelka; page 24: © Thinkstock/Elizabethb413; page 25: © Thinkstock/Carmelka; page 26: © Thinkstock/Carmelka; page 27: (hedgehog) © Thinkstock/Carmelka, (wheel) © Thinkstock/Grata Victoria; page 28: © Thinkstock/adogslifephoto; page 29: © Thinkstock/David Gallaher; pages 30–31: © Thinkstock/Catherine Yeulet; page 32: © Getty Images/Laurence Monneret.

Text copyright © 2016 by Bonnie Bader. All rights reserved. Published by Penguin Young Readers, an imprint of Penguin Random House LLC, 345 Hudson Street, New York, New York 10014. Manufactured in China.

Library of Congress Cataloging-in-Publication Data is available.

ISBN 978-0-448-48974-2 (pbk)   10 9 8 7 6 5 4 3 2 1
ISBN 978-0-448-48975-9 (hc)   10 9 8 7 6 5 4 3 2 1

PENGUIN YOUNG READERS

LEVEL
PROGRESSING
READER
2

HEDGE-HEDGEY-HEDGEHOGS

by Bonnie Bader

Penguin Young Readers
An Imprint of Penguin Random House

Is this a ball?

Is this a rock?

No!

They are hedgehogs.

Hedgehogs are small animals.

They only weigh about

one pound.

Some people keep hedgehogs in their gardens. Hedgehogs like to eat pests that live there.

A hedgehog can't see very well.

So it uses its ears to find food.

Chomp, chomp.

A snail is eating a leaf.

The hedgehog eats the snail.

A hedgehog also uses its nose

to hunt.

Sniff, sniff.

The hedgehog smells a bug.

It eats the bug in one bite.

A hedgehog can also make
a good indoor pet.
But check the laws in your town
to see if you can have one.

Be careful of your hedgehog's

sharp spines.

Put your hand under

the hedgehog.

There is fur there, not spines.

Be sure to give your hedgehog
time to get used to you.
Only hold it for
a few minutes a day.

It is not hard to take care
of a hedgehog.
It only needs about two spoons
of food a day.

You can feed your hedgehog
dry cat food.

Your hedgehog can also eat
raw or cooked meat.

A small cage makes

a good house for a hedgehog.

You can also use

a small plastic tub.

Put in a dish for food.

And a dish for water.

Or you can use a water bottle.

Put wood chips in

the bottom of the house.

Or put down paper.

You do not have to take
your hedgehog for a walk.
It will go to the bathroom
in its house.
But be sure to clean its house out
once a week!

Lick, lick.

Your hedgehog will clean itself.

Hedgehogs do not like the cold.

Be sure to put your hedgehog's

house in a warm place.

During the day, your hedgehog

will sleep curled up in a ball.

Your hedgehog will be awake at night.

Hedgehogs like to hide.
Put something in your
hedgehog's cage that
it can hide in.
Hedgehog, hedgehog,
where are you?

Hedgehogs like to play.

You can give your hedgehog

a wheel.

Run, run, run!

If you have a dog or cat,

be careful.

Your other pets may think

your hedgehog is a toy.

And their noses might get poked.

Hedgehogs should go
to the doctor.

Just like you do.

But your hedgehog

only needs to go

once a year.

Hedgehogs are cute.
Hedgehogs are tiny.
And hedgehogs can
make great pets!

OTHER LEVEL 2 BOOKS

LOOK OUT FOR **LEVEL 3** BOOKS

*Penguin Young Readers are leveled by independent reviewers applying the standards developed by Irene Fountas and Gay Su Pinnell in *Matching Books to Readers: Using Leveled Books in Guided Reading*, Heinemann, 1999.

Hedge-Hedgey-Hedgehogs

Hedgehogs are tiny animals with sharp spines.
But these cute critters make great pets!
Find out all about how to care for a hedgehog
in this fact-and-photo-filled reader.

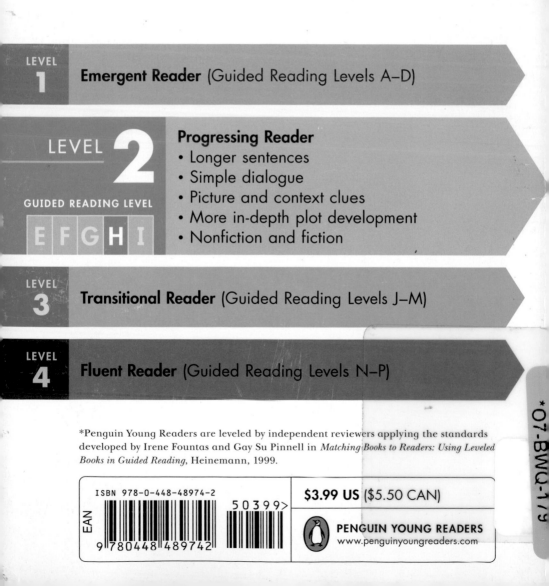

LEVEL 1

Emergent Reader (Guided Reading Levels A–D)

LEVEL 2

GUIDED READING LEVEL

E F G H I

Progressing Reader
- Longer sentences
- Simple dialogue
- Picture and context clues
- More in-depth plot development
- Nonfiction and fiction

LEVEL 3

Transitional Reader (Guided Reading Levels J–M)

LEVEL 4

Fluent Reader (Guided Reading Levels N–P)

*Penguin Young Readers are leveled by independent reviewers applying the standards developed by Irene Fountas and Gay Su Pinnell in *Matching Books to Readers: Using Leveled Books in Guided Reading*, Heinemann, 1999.

ISBN 978-0-448-48974-2

EAN

9 780448 489742

50399>

$3.99 US ($5.50 CAN)

PENGUIN YOUNG READERS
www.penguinyoungreaders.com

07-BWQ-11.9